7
Seven Wonders

Seven Wonders of
ANCIENT AFRICA

Michael Woods and Mary B. Woods

TWENTY-FIRST CENTURY BOOKS
Minneapolis

To John Starr

Twenty-First Century Books
A division of Lerner Publishing Group, Inc.
241 First Avenue North
Minneapolis, MN 55401 U.S.A.

Website address: www.lernerbooks.com

Library of Congress Cataloging-in-Publication Data

Woods, Michael, 1946–
    Seven wonders of ancient Africa / by Michael Woods and Mary B. Woods.
        p.   cm. — (Seven wonders)
    Includes bibliographical references and index.
    ISBN 978–0–8225–7571–9 (lib. bdg. : alk. paper)
    1. Architecture—Africa—Juvenile literature. 2. Architecture, Ancient—Africa—Juvenile literature. I. Woods, Mary B. (Mary Boyle),
1946– II. Title.
    NA1580.W66 2009
    722'9096—dc22   2007042104

Manufactured in the United States of America
1 2 3 4 5 6 – DP – 14 13 12 11 10 09

Contents

INTRODUCTION

*P*EOPLE LOVE TO MAKE LISTS OF THE BIGGEST AND THE BEST. ALMOST 2,500 YEARS AGO, A GREEK WRITER MADE A LIST OF THE MOST AWESOME THINGS EVER BUILT. THE LIST INCLUDED BUILDINGS, STATUES, AND OTHER OBJECTS THAT WERE LARGE, WONDROUS, AND IMPRESSIVE. OTHER ANCIENT WRITERS ADDED THEIR OWN IDEAS TO THE LIST. WRITERS EVENTUALLY AGREED ON A FINAL LIST. IT WAS CALLED THE SEVEN WONDERS OF THE ANCIENT WORLD.

THE ANCIENT WONDERS WERE:

THE GREAT PYRAMID AT GIZA: *a tomb for an ancient Egyptian king. The pyramid still stands in Giza, Egypt.*

THE COLOSSUS OF RHODES: *a giant bronze statue of Helios, the Greek sun god. The statue stood in Rhodes, an island in the Aegean Sea.*

THE LIGHTHOUSE AT ALEXANDRIA: *an enormous beacon for sailors at sea. It stood in the harbor in Alexandria, Egypt.*

THE HANGING GARDENS OF BABYLON: *magnificent gardens in the ancient city of Babylon (near modern-day Baghdad, Iraq).*

THE MAUSOLEUM AT HALICARNASSUS: *a marble tomb for a ruler in the Persian Empire. It was located in the ancient city of Halicarnassus (in modern Turkey).*

THE STATUE OF ZEUS AT OLYMPIA: *a statue honoring the king of the Greek gods. It stood in Olympia, Greece.*

THE TEMPLE OF ARTEMIS AT EPHESUS: *a temple honoring a Greek goddess. It stood on the coast of the Aegean Sea, in modern-day Turkey.*

Most of these ancient wonders are no longer standing. They were destroyed by wars, earthquakes, weather, and the passage of time.

Over the years, people made other lists of wonders. They listed wonders of the modern world and wonders of the natural world. They even listed wonders for each continent on Earth. This book is about the wonders from the continent of Africa. Like the original Seven Wonders, many of these wonders have disappeared or fallen into ruin. Modern people still study the ruins. They also learn about the wonders by studying ancient writings and pictures.

A WONDERFUL PLACE

Africa is an enormous continent. It is bigger than any continent except Asia. It is larger than the nations of China, India, the United States, and Argentina combined. Africa is home to snowcapped mountains, powerful rivers, large lakes, and other natural wonders. It is also home to millions of different kinds of plants and animals.

Scientists think that about two million years ago, the first human beings on Earth lived in Africa. At first, these early humans lived in small groups. They moved from place to place. They hunted animals and gathered wild plants for food. Eventually, humans settled down. They began living in villages. They began farming.

By about 3000 B.C., powerful rulers had taken control of some villages in Africa. These rulers created big kingdoms and built big cities. They created sculptures, monuments, and other works of art. Some of these creations were impressive and unusual. In modern times, we call them wonders.

A TRIP BACK IN TIME

Get ready to visit some of the wonders of ancient Africa. *Ancient* is another word for "old." This book will explore old cities, temples, monuments, and other creations. Some of these wonders are thousands of years old. Others date to the Middle Ages, the period between about A.D. 500 and 1500.

One chapter in this book will examine the kingdom of Aksum. There, people built gigantic tombstones. Another chapter will explore ancient Egypt and a giant monument (and a terrible monster) called the Great Sphinx. Another chapter tells about a Swiss explorer. He looked up from his path and got a surprise—a very big surprise. Get ready for more surprises as you turn the pages of this book.

THE Great Sphinx

$\mathcal{T}$HE RIDDLE OF THE SPHINX WAS

A TRICK QUESTION FROM AN ANCIENT GREEK STORY. THE STORY

TELLS OF A TERRIBLE MONSTER. IT LIVED ON A HIGH ROCK OUTSIDE

THE GREEK CITY OF THEBES. THE CREATURE WAS CALLED A SPHINX.

THE WORD *SPHINX* COMES FROM AN ANCIENT GREEK WORD

MEANING "STRANGLER."

   Sphinxes appeared in the legends and artwork of many ancient
countries. Most sphinxes had the body of a lion and the head of a human.
But some had the head of a falcon or a ram. In ancient Greece, the sphinx
had the head of a woman, the body of a lion, and the wings of an eagle.

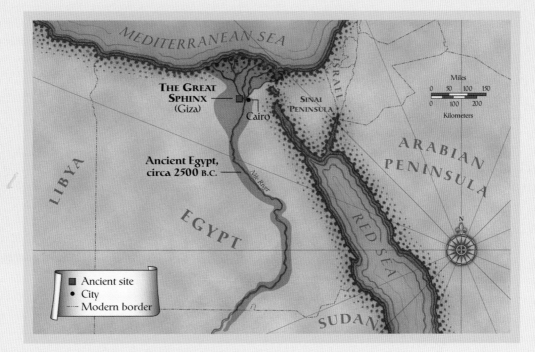

According to Greek legend, when people approached the sphinx outside Thebes, the monster stopped them and asked a riddle: "What goes on four legs in the morning, two legs at noon, and three legs in the evening?" The sphinx strangled anyone who did not answer the riddle correctly.

Nobody could figure out the riddle. Legends say that the sphinx terrified the people around Thebes. Finally, a young hero named Oedipus answered the riddle correctly. The answer was people. They crawl on hands and knees (four legs) as babies. They walk on two legs as adults. They walk on two legs and a cane (three legs) in old age. According to the legend, when the sphinx heard the answer, it became angry. It jumped off the rock to its death.

THE WORLD'S BIGGEST STONE SCULPTURE

Ancient Egypt was a kingdom in northern Africa. It flourished from about 3100 to about 1000 B.C. The ancient Egyptians told stories about sphinxes. They built thousands of statues of sphinxes in their kingdom. These statues usually had the body of a lion and the head of an ancient Egyptian king or queen.

The ancient Egyptians believed that their kings and queens were gods. Sphinxes with the heads of kings and queens reminded people that their rulers were wise and powerful.

The world's biggest and most famous sphinx is the Great Sphinx. This statue sits in the desert sands near Giza, Egypt. The Great Sphinx has the body of a lion. It has paws, claws, and a tail curled around the side. It has the head of a man.

A highway lined with nine hundred ram-headed sphinxes led to the Temple of Luxor in the ancient city of Thebes, Egypt. The sphinxes represent Amun, the Egyptian god of air and life.

The Great Sphinx was carved out of limestone by ancient Egyptians in about 2500 B.C. The giant statue, which has the body of a lion with the head of a pharaoh (king), was built along the Nile River in modern-day Giza, Egypt.

Archaeologists are people who study the remains of past cultures. Most archaeologists think that the Great Sphinx's face is a portrait of a ruler named Khafre. Khafre was an Egyptian pharaoh, or king.

The Sphinx is made of limestone. It is the largest statue on Earth carved from one block of stone. It is almost as long as a football field. It is almost as tall as a six-story building. The Great Sphinx probably was built more than forty-five hundred years ago. Its riddles still puzzle modern archaeologists. When exactly was it built? Why was it built?

RIDDLES OF THE GREAT SPHINX

Pharaoh Khafre ruled Egypt from about 2540 to about 2514 B.C. We know very little about this pharaoh. But we do know that he built giant monuments.

In addition to the Great Sphinx, Khafre built a pyramid. Egyptian pyramids were giant tombs for pharaohs and other important people. Khafre's pyramid was almost as high as a forty-seven-story building.

Khafre built his pyramid to be his tomb. But why did Khafre build the Great Sphinx? Archaeologists do not know. Khafre may have built the Great Sphinx as a monument to Horus, an Egyptian sun god. The Great Sphinx faces the east, where the sun rises. Khafre may have built the Great Sphinx to honor his own greatness. Or he might have built it to guard his pyramid.

The Great Sphinx may be the biggest stone sculpture "in the round" ever built on Earth. Sculptures in the round have three dimensions. People can walk around them and view the carvings on all sides.

The Great Sphinx's body is 238 feet (73 meters) long and 66 feet (20 m) tall. It has a face 13 feet (4 m) wide. Its eyes measure 8.5 feet (2.5 m) high. The mouth is 6.5 feet (2 m) wide. The ears are 3.3 feet (1 m) wide. The nose has broken off. It probably measured more than 5 feet (1.5 m) long. The Sphinx originally had a long, braided beard

BURIAL PLACE at Giza

Egyptian pyramids are limestone tombs for Egyptian kings. The pyramids have four triangular sides, which meet at the top to form a point. The most famous Egyptian pyramids are in Giza. In ancient times, Giza was the burial place for Egyptian royalty. The pyramids at Giza include the Great Pyramid and Pharaoh Khafre's pyramid. Smooth white stones once covered the surfaces of all the pyramids at Giza. Most of those stones fell off over the centuries. But Pharaoh Khafre's pyramid still has some of the white stones.

They pyramid of the pharaoh Khafre rises in the distance behind the Great Sphinx. It is commonly believed that Khafre built the Great Sphinx, but historians aren't sure.

A close-up view of the Great Sphinx's head reveals its missing nose. Was it destroyed by vandals? Or did it wear away over thousands of years? The mystery remains.

hanging below its chin. Nobody knows when or how the beard broke off.

The head of the Great Sphinx is carved in the shape of a royal headdress, or hat. It resembles headdresses worn by Egyptian pharaohs. In ancient times, the headdress might have had a carving of a cobra attached to the front. The top of the Sphinx's head is flat. It looks as if it was built to hold something. It has a hole where a crown or another headdress might have been attached.

Faint patches of paint still remain on the Sphinx's head. For this reason, archaeologists think the Sphinx was once painted in bright colors. Most of the paint has worn off over the centuries.

"*In front of the pyramids is the Sphinx, which is perhaps even more to be admired than they. It impresses one by its stillness and silence, and is the local divinity [god] of the inhabitants of the surrounding district.*"
—*Pliny the Elder, a Roman writer who visited Egypt in the first century A.D.*

Hieroglyphics (Egyptian picture writing) are painted and carved on many of the statues, pyramids, and temples of ancient Egypt.

BURIED IN SAND

Hieroglyphics are Egyptian picture writing. Hieroglyphics on a nearby monument say that by the 1500s B.C., windblown sand had buried the Great Sphinx up to its neck. The writing also says that an Egyptian god came to a young prince in his dream. The prince was named Thutmose. The god said that if Thutmose cleared away the sand around the Great Sphinx, he would become king of Egypt. Thutmose did clear away the sand. And his dream came true. In the 1400s B.C., he began to rule Egypt. He was called Pharaoh Thutmose IV.

Ancient Egypt declined around 1000 B.C. In the following centuries, sand again covered the Great Sphinx up to its neck. While buried, the body of the Great Sphinx was protected from more sand blowing through the air. Like the

> *"Look at me, observe me, my son [Thutmose]. I shall give to you the kingship. . . . Behold. . . . The sand of the desert, upon which I used to be [sitting], confronts [buries] me . . . and it is in order to [ask] that you do what is in my heart that I have waited."*
>
> *—Egyptian hieroglyphics, telling how a god asked Thutmose to uncover the Great Sphinx*

sand on nail files, that sand would have ground away the soft limestone of the Great Sphinx.

The French general and emperor Napoleon Bonaparte invaded Egypt in 1798. Napoleon brought a team of scientists, writers, and artists with him to Egypt. The scientists excavated, or dug around, the Great Sphinx. They removed some of the sand around the statue. The artists and writers sent drawings and stories of the Great Sphinx back to Europe. They also sent drawings and stories of Egypt's other fantastic monuments.

Giovanni Battista Caviglia was an Italian archaeologist. In 1816 he began removing the rest of the sand around the Great Sphinx. He discovered pieces of the Sphinx's broken beard. Wealthy Englishmen had provided the money for Caviglia's work. So he agreed to donate his discoveries to the British Museum in London, England. Caviglia shipped a piece of the Sphinx's beard to London for display.

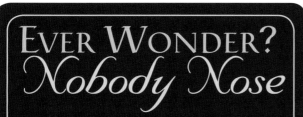

EVER WONDER?
Nobody Nose

How did the Great Sphinx lose its nose? Nobody knows. One story says that General Napoleon Bonaparte's soldiers used the monument for target practice, shooting off its nose with a cannonball. We know the story is false because in the 1600s, an Arab writer reported that the Great Sphinx's face was already damaged. Napoleon didn't arrive until later.

A MODERN WONDER

The Great Sphinx is one of modern Egypt's most famous tourist attractions. Millions of people visit it every year. Visitors can buy tickets to see this wonder up close. They enter through a

Modern Egyptian paper money features architectural wonders from Egypt's history. This bill pictures the Sphinx and the pyramids at Giza.

gate and stand at a fence for a good look at the Great Sphinx.

The pyramids and the Great Sphinx are symbols of both ancient and modern Egypt. A picture of the Great Sphinx even appears on Egypt's paper money.

In 1979 the United Nations Educational, Scientific, and Cultural Organization (UNESCO) declared the Great Sphinx and the pyramids at Giza to be a World Heritage Site. World Heritage Sites are cities, buildings, monuments, and other places that have special historical and cultural importance. UNESCO works with nations around the world to protect and preserve World Heritage Sites.

Workers have used limestone blocks to repair broken areas of the Great Sphinx. But this wonder of ancient Africa is still in danger. Blowing sand continues to eat away at the soft stone. Air pollution also damages the stone. The pollution comes from cars and industry in the nearby city of Cairo, Egypt's capital. Scientists must find new ways to protect and preserve this monster monument for future generations.

RING AROUND *the Sphinx*

Modern-day visitors will notice ridges, or rings, around the body of the Great Sphinx. These rings weren't there at first. Windblown sand striking the monument has ground away the rock. The sand has blurred the original details. It has left ridges instead.

Blowing sand has worn away the soft limestone, creating ridges around the Great Sphinx. Scientists are trying to restore and protect the Sphinx, which is one of Egypt's most popular tourist attractions.

2 Abu Simbel

$\mathcal{I}$N 1813 JOHANN BURCKHARDT WAS WALKING ALONG THE NILE RIVER IN SOUTHERN EGYPT. TO AVOID THE BRIGHT SUN, THE SWISS EXPLORER LOOKED DOWN AT THE GROUND. WHEN HE LOOKED UP AGAIN, HE COULD NOT BELIEVE HIS EYES. STICKING OUT OF THE SAND WERE STONE STATUES OF GIANT PEOPLE. "THE ENTIRE HEAD, AND PART OF THE CHEST AND ARMS OF ONE OF THE STATUES ARE ABOVE THE SURFACE," HE WROTE. "OF THE ONE NEXT TO IT SCARCELY ANY PART IS VISIBLE, THE HEAD BEING BROKEN OFF, AND THE BODY COVERED WITH SAND TO ABOVE THE SHOULDERS," HE WROTE.

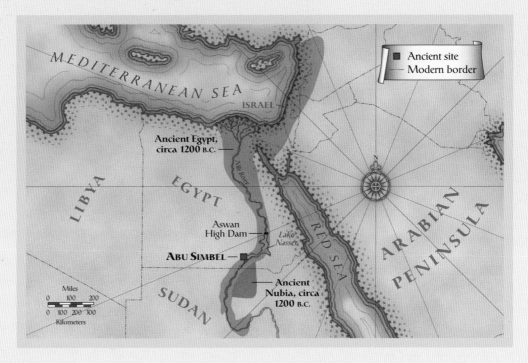

Burckhardt had discovered an ancient wonder called Abu Simbel. It consisted of two temples carved into a mountainside. Pharaoh Ramses II, who ruled Egypt in the 1200s B.C., had built the temples during his reign. An ancient inscription at the temples explains that "His Majesty commanded the making of a mansion . . . by cutting into the mountain. Never was the like done before."

RAMSES THE GREAT

Ramses II accomplished much during his years as king. He built more temples and monuments than any other pharaoh. He was also a powerful general. He protected Egypt from its enemies and conquered new lands. People called him Ramses the Great.

Ramses' soldiers fought the Hittites, who lived north of Egypt. Ramses' soldiers also fought the Nubians, who lived south of Egypt in Nubia. Abu Simbel is in southern Egypt, near Nubia. Ramses may have built his temples there to scare the Nubians. Inside the temple, wall paintings show Ramses killing Nubians during wars. Maybe Ramses built Abu Simbel to remind the Nubians that he could defeat them again.

MOUNTAINOUS CARVING

The stone at Abu Simbel is called sandstone. It is softer than most other kinds of stone. Ramses' workers could carve right into the hillside. They cut into the stone using metal saws and chisels. They built two temples. One is called the Great Temple, or Ramses' Temple.

A carving in the interior of Ramses' Temple at Abu Simbel shows the Egyptian pharaoh Ramses II conquering the Hittites in the Battle of Kadesh in the 1200s B.C. The temples probably served as a warning to the Nubians, who lived south of Egypt.

The Great Temple (left) and the Small Temple (right) were carved directly into the mountain near the banks of the Nile River in southern Egypt. Construction of the temples was begun in around 1284 B.C. and took about twenty years.

The other is the Small Temple, or Nefertari's Temple. Nefertari was Ramses' wife.

The Great Temple measures more than 100 feet (31 m) high and 120 feet (37 m) across. The temple was carved 160 feet (49 m) deep into the solid rock of the hillside. Four huge statues of Ramses guard the entrance. The statues show Ramses seated on a throne. Each statue is 67 feet (20 m) high. Inside the temple are eight more huge statues of Ramses.

Nefertari's Temple is about 82 feet (25 m) wide. It was carved 74 feet (24 m) deep into the rock. On each side of its doorway are two statues of Ramses and one of Nefertari, for a total of six statues. Each of these statues is 33 feet (10 m) high. Smaller statues show Ramses and Nefertari's children. The statues are carved so that the family seems to be walking out of the rock.

Inside, both temples contain small rooms and chambers. Both temples are decorated inside with pictures, hieroglyphics, and more statues.

Four colossal statues of Ramses II guard the entrance to the Great Temple (left). Each statue wears the double crown of Upper and Lower Egypt, signifying a pharaoh's power over all of Egypt. The kingdoms of Upper and Lower Egypt were united around 3100 B.C. The Small Temple (below) was dedicated to Ramses' wife, Nefertari. It was one of only two ancient Egyptian temples dedicated to a queen. The entrance is decorated with two groups of statues separated by a large gateway.

Artist David Roberts made this print of the inside of the Great Temple in the mid-1800s. It shows the interior of the Great Temple lined by still more statues of the pharaoh, which hadn't yet been fully uncovered from the desert sands.

A BURIED WONDER

After Ramses' death, blowing sand completely covered the Great Temple. Less sand blew on the Small Temple. It remained uncovered. Local people knew about the Small Temple. But they did not know that a larger temple was buried nearby.

People in Europe first learned about Abu Simbel after Johann Burckhardt made his discovery. A few years later, in 1817, an Italian explorer named Giovanni Battista Belzoni visited Abu Simbel. He cleared away enough sand to enter the Great Temple. "Our astonishment broke all bounds when we saw the magnificent works of art of all kinds, paintings, sculptures, colossal figures, etc., which surrounded us," Belzoni wrote.

During the 1800s and 1900s, Abu Simbel became a famous tourist attraction. People came from Europe, the United States, and other places to see the temples. Historians studied the writings and artwork inside the temples. The words and images told scholars about ancient Egyptian gods, rulers, wars, weapons, boats, clothing, musical instruments, and more.

"The whole face of the temple, as high as the heads of the statues . . . was buried in the sand which had been blown from the desert. . . . From all external appearance it is probable this temple, which is hewn out of the solid rock, had been shut. . . perhaps for more than 2,000 years."
—British travelers Charles Leonard Irby and James Mangles, describing Abu Simbel in 1823

SAVING ABU SIMBEL

After almost three thousand years, Abu Simbel almost disappeared. In the early 1960s, the government of Egypt started building a dam across the Nile River. It was called the Aswan High Dam. Egypt built the dam to prevent flooding along the Nile and to provide a steady supply of water to nearby farm fields. The dam was also built to create electric power for Egyptian cities.

When engineers dam a river, a lake forms behind the dam. The lake behind the Aswan High Dam is called Lake Nasser. It is the largest human-made lake in the world. It is 340 miles (550 kilometers) long and about 22 miles (35 km) wide. It stretches from Aswan, Egypt, past Abu Simbel, and all the way into northern Sudan.

As engineers were building the Aswan High Dam, they discovered a problem. They realized that Lake Nasser would rise and flood Abu Simbel. People needed to act fast to save this ancient wonder from the rising waters.

Scientists and engineers came up with a plan. People from around the world donated money for the project. Workers cut both temples into hundreds of huge blocks. They rebuilt the temples in a new place, safe from Lake Nasser. In the twenty-first century, the spot where Johann Burckhardt walked in 1813 is deep under Lake Nasser.

FADED *Glory*

In 1817 Percy Bysshe Shelley wrote a poem about Ramses the Great. The poem is called "Ozymandias." The British writer describes a broken statue of Ramses. Shelley calls the statue "Two vast and trunkless legs of stone . . . in the desert." The poem tells how Ramses once was great. But he ended up as just a broken statue—a "colossal Wreck, boundless and bare." What does the poem mean? Perhaps it says that even the most important people eventually lose their power. What do you think?

"The temple of Abu Simbel is not only one of the most remarkable buildings in the world, but is also a storehouse of numerous historical records carved into stone monuments at the temple."
—James H. Breasted, an American archaeologist who wrote about Abu Simbel in 1906

MIRACLE of the Sun

Ramses' Temple was built in a special position. It was placed so that on two days each year, the rising sun streamed through the entrance and lit up a statue of Ramses inside. The two days are around February 20 and October 20. Those days may have been Ramses' birth date and the date he became pharaoh. Even with the temple rebuilt in a different spot after the construction of the dam, the sun still streams into the temple around the same days each year.

A MODERN WONDER

In 1979 UNESCO named Abu Simbel and other nearby monuments to the World Heritage Site list. In the twenty-first century, Abu Simbel is one of modern Egypt's most popular tourist attractions.

An aerial view of Abu Simbel surrounded by the waters of Lake Nasser, created when the Aswan High Dam was built in Egypt in 1964. Abu Simbel was among twenty-four major monuments that were moved to safer locations. It took engineers four years to move and reassemble Abu Simbel in its new location.

3 THE KUSH Pyramids

*T*HINK OF AN ANCIENT CIVILIZATION ALONG THE BANKS OF THE NILE RIVER. THIS CIVILIZATION MUMMIFIED, OR PRESERVED, ITS DEAD KINGS, QUEENS, AND NOBLES. IT BUILT PYRAMIDS AS TOMBS FOR THE DEAD. IT WAS VERY RICH. IT HAD A POWERFUL ARMY THAT CONQUERED SURROUNDING LANDS. WHAT KINGDOM WAS IT?

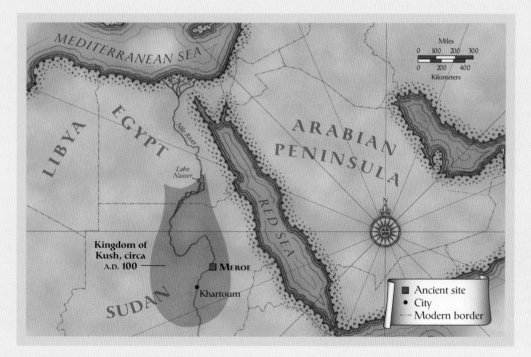

About fifty pyramids were found partly buried in the sands of Meroe, an ancient Nubian city in northern Sudan. The pyramids were burial places for Nubian kings, queens, and nobles. Meroe flourished from 300 B.C. until A.D. 300.

Ancient Egypt may come to mind. However, another advanced civilization thrived along the banks of the Nile River. That kingdom was Kush. It developed in the lands south of ancient Egypt. The kingdom lasted for almost one thousand years.

In some ways, Kush outdid Egypt. Kush had huge deposits of gold. It was much richer than Egypt. The people of Kush built about 220 pyramids—twice as many as the Egyptians did. Kush developed its own alphabet, language, and culture.

Most people, however, don't know much about Kush. The wonders of ancient Egypt, such as Abu Simbel and the Great Sphinx, have gotten much more attention.

GOLDEN *Name*

The name *Nubia* may come from the Egyptian word *nub*, which means "gold." To ancient Egyptians, Nubia was the "land of gold." It was the place that supplied gold to Egyptian pharaohs.

WONDERFUL *Archers*

Nubian warriors could shoot bows and arrows with great accuracy. Because of this, Egyptians sometimes called Nubia the Land of the Bow.

NUBIAN KINGDOMS

Ancient Kush was in a part of Africa called Nubia. Nubia includes the southern part of modern-day Egypt and the northern part of modern Sudan.

The first kingdom in Nubia developed around 2400 B.C. Over the years, this kingdom gradually expanded into southern Egypt. Egypt's rulers feared that the Nubians would take more of their land. Pharaohs wanted to block Nubian expansion. They built huge forts and walls along Egypt's southern border. War broke out between the two kingdoms around 1550 B.C. After fierce battles, Egypt conquered Nubia in 1500 B.C.

A panel from a chest buried with Egyptian king Tutankhamen in the 1300s B.C. depicts an Egyptian victory over the Nubians two hundred years earlier. Images showing Tutankhamen at war were probably symbols of his reign and power, since there is no record of wars or battles during his reign.

"Inland live the [Kushites].... They have the custom of choosing their leader according to his beauty and strength. Among them there is more gold than bronze. Accordingly they consider the scarcer metal the more precious. They adorn themselves with bronze, and make fetters [foot shackles] for the criminals from gold."

—*Pomponius Mela, a Roman geographer, A.D. 40*

The Egyptians controlled Nubia for about five hundred years. During this time, the Nubians thought of themselves as Egyptians. They dressed like Egyptians. Their homes were similar to Egyptian homes. Nubian kings and nobles lived in palaces along the Nile River. The Nubians and the Egyptians even worshipped the same gods.

In about 1000 B.C., the kingdom of Kush arose in Nubia. Around the same time, Egypt weakened. In 750 B.C., Kush took control of Egypt. Kush ruled Egypt for almost one hundred years.

In 671 B.C., the Assyrians invaded and conquered Egypt. The Kushites retreated to the south. They set up a new capital in the city of Meroe. Meroe was about 150 miles (241 km) north of Khartoum, the capital of modern Sudan.

For hundreds of years, the kingdom of Kush flourished at Meroe. In addition to gold, the area had rich deposits of iron ore. The Kushite used iron ore to make iron tools and weapons. Kush traded with Egypt and other kingdoms. Foreign merchants sold cotton, cloth, and other products to Kushite traders. The Kushites sold gold, jewels, wood, ivory (elephant tusks), iron, and other goods to foreign merchants.

ARE YOU My Mummy?

How do we know how the ancient Kushites mummified and buried their kings and queens? Paintings and carvings on the walls inside Kushite burial chambers show the process. The Kushites made a dead body into a mummy just as the Egyptians did. Priests washed the body. They removed the internal organs. They packed the body in salt to dry it. Then they wrapped the body in strips of cloth. Finally, they placed it in a coffin.

Pyramids were constructed in the Kushite city of Nuri, which reached its height between 1000 and 300 B.C. Twenty-one kings and fifty-two queens and princes are buried in Nuri. Kushite pyramids are generally 20 to 100 feet (6 to 30 m) in height. But they rise from fairly small foundations no wider than 25 feet (8 m) wide. The structures are much steeper than traditional Egyptian pyramids.

ROYAL TOMBS

The Kushites believed in life after death. When a king, queen, or other important person died, the Kushites took special steps. These steps were very similar to the ones used in Egypt. First, the Kushites turned the dead body into a mummy. Then they placed the mummy in a burial chamber inside a pyramid. They also placed food, furniture, weapons, tools, gold, jewels, and other items inside the burial chamber. The Kushites believed the dead person would need these items in the afterlife.

The Kushites built pyramids at three different cemeteries, or burial sites. The three cemeteries were at el-Kurru, Nuri, and Meroe. The Kushites began building pyramids in the 600s B.C. They built their last pyramids in the A.D. 300s. Altogether, the Kushites built more than 220 pyramids.

The interior walls of one of the pyramids at Meroe show relief (raised) carvings of Kushite life. People in early Kush used Egyptian hieroglyphics, but people in Meroe developed a new script in the 300s B.C. They began to write the Meroitic language, which has not been fully deciphered.

Like the Egyptians, the Kushites built their pyramids from stone blocks. However, Kushite pyramids were narrower, with steeper sides. We do not know how the Kushites built their pyramids. But they were probably easier to build than Egyptian pyramids because they were smaller. Kushite pyramids range from 20 to 100 feet (6 to 30 m) tall. By comparison, some Egyptian pyramids are more than 400 feet (122 m) tall. Smaller pyramids required fewer stone blocks, fewer workers, and less time to build.

CURTAINS FOR KUSH

Iron making was an important industry for Kush. The Kushites made iron in hot furnaces. They needed firewood to fuel the furnaces. They got the firewood by cutting down trees. Archaeologist think the Kushites cut down trees faster than new trees could grow. By the A.D. 300s, the Kushites had run out of firewood. The iron industry began to suffer.

Cutting down trees hurt Kush in another way. Tree roots hold soil in place. When the Kushites cut down trees, the soil became loose. It washed away in the rain. Without good soil, it was hard for farmers to grow food.

As iron making and farming declined, Kush began to lose strength and wealth. The kingdom ended in about A.D. 350.

European artist Max Schmidt painted this scene of the pyramids at Meroe in 1840. (The painting was reproduced as a black-and-white engraving shown above.)

SAVING ANCIENT KUSH

Over the next one thousand years, various groups ruled Nubia and the lands that had once been Kush. Local people knew about the pyramids and other Kushite treasures, but the ancient kingdom was forgotten.

In the 1820s, Egypt conquered Nubia and other parts of northern Sudan. Around the same time, British, French, and American travelers began to arrive in Nubia. These travelers told the world about the pyramids and other remains of ancient Kush. The British took control of Sudan in the late 1800s. In the following decade, an American archaeologist began to excavate the pyramids and other Kushite ruins.

In modern times, northern Nubia sits under the waters of Lake Nasser. Before the lake filled with water, people rescued Abu Simbel from the floodwaters. They also rescued some Kushite temples, tombs, tools, weapons, pottery, and other items. The rescuers rebuilt some of the big structures on higher ground. They sent the smaller items to museums around the world. However, other wonders of ancient Kush were covered with water. Some may forever remain a mystery.

The southern portions of ancient Kush were not flooded. Archaeologists have studied this region to learn more about the kingdom of Kush. This work is not easy. In the late twentieth century, groups in Sudan began to fight one another. By the early 2000s, southern Sudan was too dangerous for archaeologists to visit. It is also too dangerous for tourists. Until war ends in the region, few people will be able to visit the pyramids and other remains of ancient Kush.

TREASURE *Hunters*

In the 1830s, a doctor named Giuseppe Ferlini worked with the Egyptian army in Sudan. During his stay, he also explored the pyramids at Meroe. He knocked the tops off many pyramids *(below)*, looking for treasures hidden inside. Finally, Ferlini discovered gold rings, necklaces, and other jewelry in one of the pyramids. People soon told stories about the fantastic "Ferlini treasure." The stories attracted other treasure hunters.

Historians think that Ferlini gave false information about his discovery. To mislead other treasure hunters, he said the riches came from a secret chamber at the top of the pyramid. In fact, he probably found the treasure in a burial chamber beneath the pyramid. Because of Ferlini's lie, other treasure hunters also knocked the peaks off Kushite pyramids. As a result, many pyramids at Meroe are missing their peaks.

This redware ceramic bowl (right) was made by the Kushites in about 600 B.C. Below: Camels and a rider cross the desert sands at Meroe.

4 THE KINGDOM OF *Aksum*

The queen of Sheba (kneeling) visits King Solomon (seated on throne). German painter Hans Memling created this illustration in the 1400s. It appeared in a prayer book known as the Grimani Breviary.

STORIES SAY THAT THE QUEEN

OF SHEBA WAS THE WORLD'S RICHEST AND WISEST WOMAN. HER

KINGDOM, SHEBA, WAS IN NORTHEASTERN AFRICA. ONE DAY THE

QUEEN HEARD ABOUT THE WORLD'S RICHEST AND WISEST MAN.

HE WAS KING SOLOMON. HE RULED FAR AWAY IN JERUSALEM,

IN MODERN-DAY ISRAEL.

The queen decided to visit Solomon. She traveled to the kingdom of Jerusalem with gold and other gifts for Solomon. The queen and Solomon married and had a son. He took the name Menelik, which means "son of the wise." He ruled Sheba after his mother's death. His children and their descendants later became rulers of Sheba.

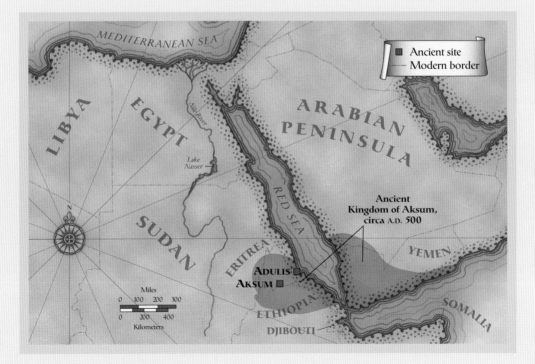

> *"From that place to the city of the people called Auxumites [Aksum] there is a five days' journey more; to that place all the ivory is brought from the country beyond the Nile through the district called Cyeneum, and thence to Adulis."*
>
> ——The Periplus of the Erythraean Sea, *a guide written for sailors in about A.D. 100*

Nobody knows if the stories about the queen of Sheba are true. However, people in Africa and other places still tell these stories thousands of years later. Holy books of the Christian, Islamic, and Jewish religions mention the queen of Sheba. In the twentieth century, Emperor Haile Selassie ruled the African nation of Ethiopia. He said that he was descended from Solomon and the queen of Sheba.

AKSUM, PERHAPS?

Who was the queen of Sheba? Where was her kingdom? No one is sure. But she might have ruled the kingdom of Aksum in northeastern Africa. Aksum was the name of the kingdom and its capital city.

The kingdom of Aksum emerged about A.D. 100. At first, it covered lands that would become modern-day Eritrea and northern Ethiopia. Aksum's armies conquered other lands. The kingdom expanded. By A.D. 500, Aksum included a large area. It extended from the modern nation of Sudan in the west to the modern nation of Yemen in the east. It reached south into modern-day Somalia.

Aksum was a perfect trading center. It had a port city called Adulis. The city sat on the Red Sea, which lies between northeastern Africa and the Arabian Peninsula. Merchants bought gold, jewels, ivory, and spices from deep inside Africa.

EVER WONDER?
The Kings' Clothes

How do we know about the rulers of Aksum? Coins from that ancient kingdom were imprinted with the names and images of more than twenty different kings. The images show the clothing that some of the kings wore.

They carried these goods to Adulis. Then they shipped the goods across the sea to markets in Rome, Greece, Arabia, India, and other lands. The ships returned to Adulis loaded with silver, gold, olive oil, and wine from these far-off places.

SKYSCRAPER TOMBSTONES

Aksum's rulers built palaces and temples. They built tombs for themselves and their families. Their most fantastic buildings were stelae. These were tall, thin, four-sided stone monuments. Stelae marked the location of royal tombs. These giant tombstones look a lot like the Washington Monument in the U.S. capital of Washington, D.C. Aksum had more than one hundred stelae.

Other ancient civilizations, including ancient Egypt, also built stelae. But Aksum's stelae were unusual. For one thing, they were bigger than stelae in other places. The biggest stela from Aksum is called Stela 1. In modern times, the stela is broken and lies on the ground. But when standing, it would have been 97 feet (30 m) high. The stela's base measures 12.5 feet (3.8 m) by 7.9 feet (2.4 m).

Aksum's stelae were also unusual in their design. Workers carved the sides of stelae to look like buildings. The sides show outlines of doors, windows, and even the ends of "wooden" beams.

> *"In the tomb many grave goods still remained [after tomb robbers had broken in]. There were fragments of gold and silver jewelry, beads, bronze objects . . . iron weapons, exquisite glassware, goblets and flasks, beautifully decorated pots."*
> —archaeologist Stuart Munro-Hay, who excavated a tomb at Aksum in the 1970s

Stela 1 is carved to look like a building with thirteen stories. Archaeologists think the stelae were supersize versions of the palaces where kings, queens, and nobles lived in Aksum.

Aksum's stelae are monoliths. That means they were cut from single pieces of stone (*mono* means "one," and *lith* means "stone"). By contrast, the Washington Monument was built from many small blocks of stone. They are

A close-up photo of the stela marking King Ezana's tomb looks like a modern-day skyscraper. King Ezana, who ruled during the A.D. 300s, was the first monarch in Aksum to adopt Christianity.

stacked one on top of the other. When it was standing, Stella 1 may have been the world's tallest monolith.

Many of Aksum's stelae were built by King Ezana. He ruled Aksum from about A.D. 320 to 356. The stela marking Ezana's tomb is the highest one still standing at Aksum. It is 70 feet (21 m) tall.

A WONDER *Returned*

Italy invaded Ethiopia in 1935. The Italians took one of Aksum's famous stelae back to Italy. They set up the 80-foot-high (24 m) stela in the capital city of Rome. To the Italians, the stela was a symbol of victory. But Ethiopia saw the stela as a symbol of its ancient heritage. In the late 1940s, Ethiopia asked Italy to give the stela back. But Italy kept stalling. Finally, in 2005, Italy returned the monument to Ethiopia *(below)*.

WONDERING ABOUT THE WORK

Rock is heavy. A small stone block just 1 foot (0.3 m) on each side weighs about 160 pounds (73 kilograms). Stela 1 weighs about 520 *tons* (472 metric tons, or more than 1 million pounds). The quarries with rock for stelae were about 3 miles (4 km) away from the city of Askum. How did people who had no modern machines cut such big slabs of rock from the ground? How did workers move such huge and heavy blocks of stone? How did they lift them upright?

Workers probably used iron tools to scratch an outline of a stela into rock in the quarry. Then they cut slots into the lines. By pounding metal wedges into those slots, workers split the rock. Little by little, workers made the split longer and deeper. Finally, the entire slab of rock came loose.

We do not know how workers moved the heavy slabs to Aksum.

They may have used logs as rollers. They may have placed a slab of rock on top of logs and pulled it. Perhaps elephants pulled the slab. As the rock moved slowly down the road, its front section would have rolled off the logs. Workers constantly had to move logs from the back to the front. In this way, logs always supported the full length of the rock.

Oops!

When the slab arrived in Aksum, workers finished the design. They used iron chisels to smooth and carve the sides. To raise the stela upright, workers probably dug a hole in the ground. They placed the base of the slab over the hole. Then they attached ropes to the top of the stela. They pulled on the ropes to raise the structure. With more pulling, the bottom of the stela settled deep into the hole. The rock monument rose upright.

Rock may seem strong. But long pieces of rock can crack easily. We can only guess at how many stclac broke on the way to Aksum or while being raised upright. Stela 1 might have broken right after workers raised it. Or it might have broken later.

In the late 600s, warfare increased on the Red Sea. The fighting interfered with trade. With less trade, Aksum grew weaker. In the 700s, Arab invaders conquered the port city of Adulis. Aksum could no longer trade by sea. Aksum weakened even more in the 800s. By the 900s, the kingdom had ended.

THE ARK at Aksum?

The Bible is a collection of writings from the ancient Middle East. Some parts of the Bible are sacred to both Christians and Jews. Other parts are sacred to just Christians. The Bible describes a wooden chest called the Ark of the Covenant. According to the Bible, the ark contained stone tablets inscribed with the Ten Commandments. The commandments were God's rules for living and worship. The Bible says that King Solomon kept the ark at his temple in Jerusalem. In 586 B.C., the Babylonians destroyed Solomon's temple. No one knows what happened to the ark after that. One legend says that the ark was smuggled into Aksum. Most historians don't believe this story.

A Modern Wonder

Modern Aksum is a city in Ethiopia. It is home to about thirty thousand people. In 1980 UNESCO listed the city of Aksum as a World Heritage Site. Modern visitors to the city can still see walls, buildings, stelae, and other ruins from ancient times.

Like most Ethiopians, the people of Aksum are very poor. Summer rains sometimes wash gold, silver, and bronze coins of ancient Aksum out of the soil. These ancient treasures remind Aksum's residents of their city's former greatness.

These stelae are located in the Gudit Stela Field near Aksum. The Gudit Stelae Field is named after Queen Gudit, who conquered Aksum in the tenth century A.D.

5 THE Swahili Coast

The ruins of a palace overlook the Indian Ocean from the island of Kilwa. The palace was built out of coral stone in the 1400s by Sultan (king) al-Hasan ibn Sulaiman, a descendent of the Arab rulers of Kilwa. The palace included more than one hundred rooms and terraces but was abandoned before it was completed.

*I*N 1497 VASCO DA GAMA LEFT PORTUGAL WITH A FLEET OF FOUR SHIPS. THE PORTUGUESE SEA CAPTAIN WAS TRYING TO FIND A SEA ROUTE TO ASIA, SOMETHING THAT EUROPEANS HAD NEVER DONE BEFORE.

From Portugal, da Gama's ships headed south. They sailed along the western coast of Africa. In late 1497, the ships sailed around the southern tip of Africa. They turned north and headed into the Indian Ocean. As da Gama traveled north, he saw an amazing sight. One after another, he found a string of wealthy cities along the coast of East Africa.

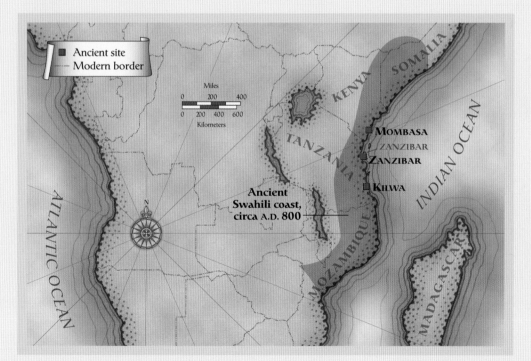

A historian named Gaspar Correa traveled with da Gama on that voyage. He wrote about one of the cities: "The city comes down to the shore, and is entirely surrounded by a wall and towers, within which there are maybe 12,000 inhabitants. The country all round is very luxurious with many trees and gardens of all sorts of vegetables, citrons, lemons, and the best sweet oranges that were ever seen. . . . The houses are very high, of three and four stories . . . and in the port there were many ships."

ANCIENT SHOPPING MALL

The city that Correa wrote about was Kilwa (in modern-day Tanzania). Kilwa was one of more than thirty trading and fishing settlements on the east coast of Africa when the Portuguese arrived. Other settlements were Mombasa (in modern-day Kenya) and Zanzibar (on the island of Zanzibar).

CANANOR

DE GESCHIEDENIS VAN INDIE.
11. Vasco de Gama te Cananor.

In the late 1400s, Vasco da Gama (right) and his crew were the first Europeans to sail around the eastern coast of Africa. Below: This engraving, done nearly four hundred years later, shows Zanzibar still flourishing with trade.

These settlements were part of a rich trading network called the Swahili coast.

The Swahili coast was like a huge ancient shopping mall—with thousands of items for sale. The coastal settlements stretched for almost 1,800 miles (2,897 km), about the distance from New York City to Denver, Colorado. The coastal inhabitants were the Swahili people. They shared a language and culture.

The Swahili coast surprised da Gama. But before he arrived, trading ships had been coming to the Swahili coast for more than one thousand years. Around A.D. 100, a Greek trader wrote a guide for sailors. The guide describes the Swahili coast as a well-known center for trade. "Men of the greatest stature [status] . . . inhabit the whole coast and at each place have set up chiefs," the guide states.

I'LL TRADE YOU

In ancient times, when merchants needed goods to sell, they had to travel to get them. Sometimes they traveled by ship. Other times they traveled overland. On land, merchants used camels and other pack animals to carry heavy loads.

Certain goods were precious to ancient people. These goods included iron, gold, ivory, pearls, salt, animal skins, and tortoiseshells. The Swahili coast was one of the best places to get such precious goods. Merchants could also buy slaves on the Swahili coast.

"Two days' sail beyond the island lies the last mainland market town of Azania, which is called Rhapta, a name derived from the small sewn boats the people use. Here there is much ivory and tortoiseshell."

—The Periplus of the Erythraean Sea, *A.D. 100*

"*[The Aksum traders] lay the pieces [of slaughtered oxen] on the top of the [fence], along with the lumps of salt and the iron. Then come the natives bringing gold in nuggets like peas . . . and lay [them] upon what pleases them. . . . Then the owner of the meat [or salt or iron] approaches and if he is satisfied he takes the gold away, and upon seeing this [the owner of the gold] comes and takes the flesh or the salt or the iron.*"

—*a Greek merchant, describing how people traded goods on the Swahili coast in the 700s*

Ships came to Kilwa and other ports from Greece, Rome, Arabia, China, and India. These ships carried loads of pepper, silk, fine cloth, glass, rice, and perfumes. At the same time, African merchants traveled to the Swahili coast from kingdoms in the interior of Africa. They brought gold, iron, ivory, animal hides, slaves, and other trade goods from their own lands. At the coast, merchants from different lands made trades. For instance, an African merchant might swap gold or ivory for fine cloth and perfumes from Arabia.

Kilwa Kisiwani was the richest city in eastern Africa from 1000 to 1500. This bird's-eye view of the city was pubished in 1572 in a world atlas known as the Civitates Orbis Terrarum (*cities of the world*) *in Cologne, Italy.*

46

TRADERS AND CONQUERORS

In the early years of the first century A.D., a group of Bantu-speaking people ruled the Swahili coast. They controlled the coastal trade. In about A.D. 200, people from Persia (modern-day Iran) took over the coastal trade. Later, people from Arabia took control.

In ancient times, merchant ships were sailboats. They relied on the wind to drive them from place to place. When ships arrived on the Swahili coast, they often had to stay there for several months. Sailors had to wait for the wind to change direction and blow them home.

While waiting for the winds to change, Arab traders lived among the local Bantu people for long periods. During these long stays, the Arabs introduced their culture to the Swahili coast. They introduced their religion, Islam. Many local people adopted this religion. Local people began worshipping in mosques,

This mosque was built on the island of Kilwa Kisiwani, off the coast of Tanzania. It is the oldest remaining mosque on the East African coast. The original structure has a foundation that dates back to the 900s. But people continued to renovate and add on to the mosque into the 1300s.

or Islamic temples. In their home countries, Arabs shopped in open-air markets called bazaars. Soon, traders built bazaars in Kilwa and other cities on the Swahili coast.

Traders and local people spoke different languages. The Arabs introduced some of their words to the Swahili coast. In fact, the name *Swahili* comes from an Arabic term, *sahil*, which means "coast." People also mixed words from Arabic, Bantu, Persian, and other languages to create a new language. This language is called Swahili, or Kiswahili. It has a beautiful, musical sound. Some Arab men married Bantu-speaking women. Their children were the first of a new people, the Swahili people.

During his visit, Vasco da Gama marveled at the wealth of the Swahili coast. He claimed the coast as new territory for the king of Portugal. Portugal sent warships to conquer the area. Portugal ruled the Swahili coast for about two hundred years.

The Arabs recaptured Zanzibar in 1698. They also took back other parts of the coast. In the following centuries, various European nations controlled different parts of the Swahili coast. In the twentieth century, the nations of East Africa finally gained independence.

TRADING for Tusks

Traders came to the Swahili coast to buy ivory. This hard, white material makes up the tusks of elephants and some other animals. Ivory is very valuable. It is pure white. It is very strong, yet it is easy to carve. In ancient times, craftspeople carved ivory into statues, jewelry, and other objects.

A MODERN WONDER

In modern times, the Swahili coast is divided into the nations of Somalia, Kenya, Tanzania, and Mozambique. These countries are home to many ethnic groups, including about 500,000 Swahili people. At least 60 million people in East Africa speak Kiswahili.

Some of the wonders of the ancient Swahili coast remain in modern times. People can visit modern Zanzibar, Mombasa, Kilwa, and other cities and see their ancient heritage. One historic site is the Great Mosque of Kilwa. It was built in the late 1100s or early 1200s. It was once the largest mosque on the

East African coast. Visitors to Kilwa also can see the Great House. It was once the home of a fifteenth-century sultan, or ruler. Another tourist attraction is Stone Town in Zanzibar City. It is a historic area, with many houses, shops, and mosques from ancient times.

Both Kilwa and Stone Town are listed as UNESCO World Heritage Sites. The Swahili coast is no longer a gigantic shopping mall. But it is still a wondrous place to visit.

Zanzibar as it looked in the 1800s (below) *and in modern times* (right)

GREAT Zimbabwe

*I*N THE EARLY 1500S, MANY PORTUGUESE TRADERS LIVED ALONG THE COAST OF SOUTHERN AFRICA. LOCAL PEOPLE TOLD THE TRADERS AMAZING STORIES ABOUT MYSTERIOUS "LOST CITIES." ACCORDING TO THE STORIES, THESE CITIES HAD ONCE TEEMED WITH PEOPLE. ONE CITY HAD A MAGNIFICENT STONE PALACE BRIMMING WITH GOLD, JEWELS, AND OTHER TREASURE. LOCAL PEOPLE SAID THAT THE CITIES HAD BEEN ABANDONED MANY YEARS BEFORE.

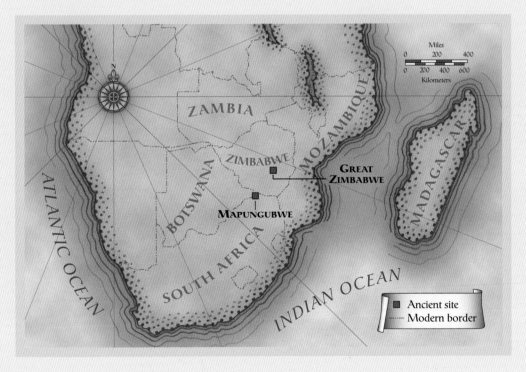

"I do not think that I am wrong if [I] suppose that the . . . building in the plain [is] a copy of the palace where the Queen of Sheba lived during her visit to Solomon."

—nineteenth-century German archaeologist Karl Mauch, one of many Europeans who thought Africans had not built Great Zimbabwe

The Portuguese traders weren't sure if the stories were true. Then they made a fantastic discovery. They found an enormous walled city in the south of modern-day Zimbabwe. The city contained stone walls and buildings. It also contained a big stone palace. The city had enough room for seven thousand homes.

The Europeans didn't know who had made the city. Some thought it was part of the queen of Sheba's ancient kingdom. Others thought the ancient Egyptians, Chinese, or Phoenicians had built the city.

The Europeans were wrong. The city was Great Zimbabwe. It had not been built thousands of years earlier by people from thousands of miles away. It had been built just a few hundred years earlier by people living in the area. Eventually, Great Zimbabwe became one of southern Africa's greatest symbols of pride.

BUILT TO LAST

Who built Great Zimbabwe? The builders were probably the Shona people. The Shona came to power in southern Africa around A.D. 1100. They ruled the area around Great Zimbabwe until the mid-1400s. They built their great city during these years. The name *Zimbabwe* is a Shona word. Scholars aren't certain what it means. It may mean "stone house," "place of the king," or "sacred house."

Great Zimbabwe has three main sections. The acropolis, or Hill Ruins, is the city's oldest section. This area has stone buildings and twisting passageways on a hill. The Hill Ruins were probably royal buildings where the rulers of Great Zimbabwe lived.

The Great Enclosure is the second section. Here is the stone castle that so impressed Portuguese traders in the 1500s. The Great Enclosure also has two cone-shaped towers. The biggest one is 36 feet (11 m) high.

Above: *The Great Enclosure and the Valley Ruins of the city of Great Zimbabwe would have housed thousands of people between the twelfth and fifteenth centuries.* Left: *One of the two cone-shaped towers inside the Great Enclosure*

The ruins of living quarters are here too. Each household has the remains of two huts, a kitchen, and a small courtyard surrounded by a stone wall. A big oval wall surrounds the Great Enclosure. The wall is more than 800 feet (244 m) long, 32 feet (10 m) high, and 17 feet (5 m) thick.

The third section of Great Zimbabwe is called the Valley Ruins. It was built in a nearby valley. The valley holds more ruins of stone walls and huts.

Left: *An aerial view of Great Zimbabwe. The word Zimbabwe might mean "house of stone." The modern country is called Zimbabwe in honor of the civilization that built these stone structures.* Right: *This photo shows how tightly the bricks were placed together. The tall walls were built without mortar.*

The structures at Great Zimbabwe were built to last. The huts in the Great Enclosure were made from a mixture of wet clay and small stones. When it dried, the mixture became as hard as concrete. The wall around the Great Enclosure was built from blocks of granite, a heavy stone. The blocks were cut with amazingly flat sides. Each block fit snugly against the next. The fit is so tight that builders did not need mortar to hold the blocks together.

"Among the gold mines of the inland plains between the Limpopo and Zambezi rivers [there is a] . . . fortress built of stones of marvelous size, and there appears to be no mortar joining them. . . . This edifice [building] is almost surrounded by hills, upon which are others resembling it in the fashioning of stone and the absence of mortar."
—*Vicente Pegado, a Portuguese soldier who wrote about Great Zimbabwe in 1531*

OTHER LOST CITIES: *The Kingdom of the Golden Rhino*

Great Zimbabwe was one of several "lost cities" of southern Africa. Another was the city of Mapungubwe, in the modern nation of South Africa. The city thrived from about A.D. 1000 to 1300.

Mapungubwe may have had five thousand residents at its peak. These city dwellers traded gold, ivory, and other goods with people as far away as India and China. Farmers in Mapungubwe raised cattle, grain, and cotton. Artists there made jewelry from gold, ivory, and shells. Craftspeople fashioned weapons and other objects from iron and copper.

Archaeologists discovered the ruins of Mapungubwe in 1932. Among the ruins, they uncovered some royal graves. In one grave, they found an artifact (remains) called the Golden Rhino. It was a small wooden rhinoceros. It was covered with sheets of gold, held in place with tiny tacks.

The archaeologist knew that Mapungubwe was an important civilization created by black Africans. But the white rulers of South Africa believed that blacks were inferior to whites. They ordered the archaeologists to keep information about Mapungubwe a secret. Eventually, more people learned about Mapungubwe. Along with Great Zimbabwe, the city became a symbol of the skills and creativity of black Africans.

RISE AND FALL OF A GREAT CITY

In the 1400s, Great Zimbabwe was home to about twenty thousand people. In those days, a city with twenty thousand people was enormous.

Great Zimbabwe was far from other cities, such as those on the Swahili coast. How did such a big city arise in this remote area of Africa? How did its many residents get their food? Soil in the area was poor. Growing large amounts of food would have been difficult.

The Shona left no written records. Archaeologists can only guess at the answers to these questions. One idea involves gold. The area around Great Zimbabwe has large deposits of gold. Some archaeologists think the Shona built Great Zimbabwe as a place to process and store this precious metal. Great Zimbabwe may also have been a trading center, where merchants exchanged food for gold and other goods.

By the time Portuguese explorers reached Great Zimbabwe, it had been abandoned. Archaeologists think the people left in the mid-1400s. But we do not know why they left. Perhaps the Shona had mined all the gold nearby. Or maybe the city got too big. Maybe people couldn't grow enough food to feed everyone or couldn't collect enough firewood for cooking and heating. Perhaps merchants found trading centers that were richer and easier to reach. Without enough traders, Great Zimbabwe could no longer get all the goods it needed. People may have left Great Zimbabwe for any or all of these reasons.

BACK TO LIFE

For hundreds of years, Great Zimbabwe remained a mystery. Many white Europeans refused to believe that black Africans had built Great Zimbabwe. In earlier centuries, many Europeans thought that black people were not smart enough or skilled enough to build cities.

In the 1930s, archaeologists carefully studied tools, pottery, and other artifacts (remains) from Great Zimbabwe. They saw that the items were identical to artifacts made by the Shona people in other areas. They found no hint that anyone from other lands had ever lived or worked in Great Zimbabwe. These studies proved that Africans had built Great Zimbabwe. Great Zimbabwe became a symbol of the knowledge, skills, and achievements of southern African people.

GREAT BIRDS OF *Great Zimbabwe*

Great Zimbabwe's most famous artifacts are eight birds carved out of stone. The birds are about 16 inches (41 centimeters) high. They mostly look like birds. But they have human feet instead of claws and lips instead of beaks. Archaeologists think the birds were symbols of the royal families that once ruled Great Zimbabwe.

EVER WONDER?
Great Traders

How do archaeologists know that Great Zimbabwe traded with distant lands? Excavations at Great Zimbabwe have uncovered glass beads made in ancient China and a coin used in Arabia in the 1300s. These artifacts are clues that merchants in Great Zimbabwe traded with faraway countries.

For much of the twentieth century, the British ruled the area around Great Zimbabwe. The British called the territory Rhodesia. Rhodesia gained independence from Great Britain in 1980.

Local people wanted a new name for their country. They decided to name it after Great Zimbabwe. They named it

A group of British nobility, including the mother of Queen Elizabeth II, visited the ruins at Great Zimbabwe in 1953 when Great Britain ruled the area.

the Republic of Zimbabwe. People created a new flag for their country. The flag has green, yellow, red, and black stripes. It also has a picture of a bird. The bird is modeled after carved stone birds found at Great Zimbabwe.

A MODERN WONDER

The ruins of Great Zimbabwe still stand. In 1986 UNESCO added the ruins to the World Heritage Site list. The ruins are in a park called Great Zimbabwe National Monument. Visitors can enter the park and walk among the stone walls and buildings.

The Shona people still live in the area around Great Zimbabwe. They make up about 80 percent of modern Zimbabwe's population. The Shona are proud of their ancient heritage and the great city built by their ancestors.

These girls are modern-day Shona. They live in the Manicanaland Province in eastern Zimbabwe. Their ancestors built the city of Great Zimbabwe.

The ruins of Great Zimbabwe cover an area of nearly 200 acres (80 hectares). Great Zimbabwe was an important trading center during its time and is a major tourist attraction in modern-day Zimbabwe.

7 Timbuktu

The Sankore Mosque in Timbuktu, Mali, was built in the 1500s. Also known as the University of Sankore, the mosque was one of three learning centers that made up the University of Timbuktu. Timbuktu attracted Islamic scholars from across the Muslim world.

*H*AVE YOU EVER HEARD THE EXPRESSION, "ALL THE WAY TO TIMBUKTU"? PEOPLE SOMETIMES USE THIS EXPRESSION WHEN THEY'RE TALKING ABOUT A PLACE THAT'S FAR AWAY AND HARD TO REACH. TO SOME PEOPLE, TIMBUKTU SEEMS LIKE THAT KIND OF PLACE. IT SEEMS LIKE THE END OF THE EARTH.

But Timbuktu is not the end of the earth. It is a city in the western African country of Mali. For hundreds of years, ancient Timbuktu was a place of fantastic wonders and wealth. In the 1300s, Timbuktu was a great center for trade, learning, religion, and culture.

Timbuktu was also a city of riches. Gold traders came to Timbuktu from other places in western Africa. The gold trade made Timbuktu richer than London, Paris, and other famous European cities.

At its height, ancient Timbuktu had a population of about one hundred thousand people. It had splendid palaces, two universities, and large libraries with thousands of manuscripts. Timbuktu was a center of Islamic learning. It had about 180 Islamic schools, with twenty-five thousand students. Because of its splendor, Timbuktu was called the Pearl of Africa.

A WONDER FROM A WELL

Most experts think that Timbuktu began in the A.D. 1100s. In that century, a woman named Bouctou opened a rest stop for merchants traveling with their goods and camels. The rest stop included a well.

Above: *An artist in the 1600s depicted Timbuktu, Mali. The city had reached its height one hundred years earlier as an intellectual and trading center.* Below: *A caravan (group) of Arab traders and their camels crosses a stream in the Sahara desert. Traders came from all over the region to trade salt, gold, slaves, and ivory.*

> *"Salt comes from the north, gold from the south, and silver from the country of the white men, but the word of God and the treasures of wisdom are only to be found in Timbuktu."*
>
> —western African saying

That's how the place got its name: *tim Bouctou* meant "the well of Bouctou" in the language of the local people. The modern spelling is Timbuktu or Tombouctou.

Timbuktu is on the edge of the Sahara desert. Timbuktu is about 8 miles (12 km) north of the Niger River. For hundreds of years, traders met in this area. Some traders came overland from the north and the east. Others traveled by boats along the Niger River. Yet other traders came from forests in lands to the south.

The southern merchants brought gold to Timbuktu. Northern merchants brought salt from salt mines to the north. In addition to gold and salt, traders also swapped ivory, animal skins, bars of iron, and slaves at Timbuktu.

LION KINGS

At first the western African trade routes were part of the kingdom of Ghana. Ghana was the area's first great empire. It thrived between the A.D. 700s and mid-1000s.

Al-Bakri, a Spanish writer, lived in the 1000s. He described the power and wealth of Ghana's ruler: "The king of Ghana when he calls up his

EVER WONDER?
Great Griots

In ancient times, people in some parts of Africa did not have writing systems. Without written records, how do we know about the history of Africa's early kingdoms? Before there was written language, people spread information through pictures, stories, and songs.

Some people were griots, or professional storytellers. Griots memorized history, stories, poems, sayings, and songs. They passed on their knowledge by reciting the songs and stories to the younger generation. Younger griots memorized and recited the same information and on and on through the generations.

army, can put 200,000 men into the field, more than 40,000 of them archers. The king . . . sits in audience . . . in a domed pavilion around which stand ten horses covered with gold-embroidered materials. Behind the king stand ten pages holding shields and swords decorated with gold, and on his right are the sons of the [leaders] of his country wearing splendid garments and their hair plaited with gold."

Ghana collapsed in A.D. 1076. In about 1235, a great leader named Sundiata united people of the region into the area's second great empire. It was the empire of Mali. Sundiata was a strong leader. People called him the Lion King. Under Sundiata, Mali grew rich and powerful.

THE WORLD'S RICHEST KING

A man named Mansa Musa became ruler of Mali in 1307. Mansa Musa amassed a huge army. His soldiers conquered nearby lands. Mali doubled in size. Many gold mines were on those conquered lands. With the extra gold, Mali grew even richer.

Mansa Musa was a Muslim, a follower of the Islamic religion. At least once in a lifetime, Muslims try to make a trip to Mecca. Mecca is a holy city in the modern country of Saudi Arabia. In 1324 Mansa Musa began his trip to Mecca. He started from a small city southwest of Timbuktu. The distance was more than 3,000 miles (4,827 km).

Mansa Musa traveled like the great king that he was. He took thousands of servants, slaves, friends, family members, soldiers, and others along on the journey. Hundreds of camels carried food, water, clothing, tents, and everything else the group needed to live.

One hundred of the camels had a special cargo. They each carried 300 pounds (136 kg) of gold. Mansa Musa gave away the gold along the route to Mecca. He told people the gold was from Timbuktu.

After the trip, stories about the richness of Mali and Timbuktu spread around the world. In 1375 a mapmaker in Spain made a map of the known

"The richest and noblest King in the world"
—a Spanish description of Mansa Musa, 1375

A map made by a Spanish mapmaker in 1375 shows King Mansa Musa of Timbuktu sitting on a golden throne, wearing a gold crown, and holding a gold nugget and scepter. The wealth of Timbuktu and Mansa Musa became widely known after his famous journey to Mecca, Saudi Arabia, that started in 1324.

world. The map showed Mansa Musa in western Africa. He sat on a throne, holding a nugget of gold. The map described him as the world's richest king.

BACK TO TIMBUKTU

When Mansa Musa returned to western Africa, he brought scholars back from Egypt. He encouraged scholars from other countries to move to Timbuktu. Mansa Musa built a great palace, a mosque, schools, and other buildings in Timbuktu. By the end of his reign, Timbuktu was a wealthy city and a center of Islamic learning.

In the 1400s, another kingdom emerged in western Africa. It grew into the powerful Songhai Empire. Songhai armies began to invade parts of Mali. In

1468 Songhai conquered Timbuktu. By 1500 the empire of Mali had ended. Traders forgot about Timbuktu. They took their business to the Swahili coast and other African trading centers. After the traders left, Timbuktu became a poor and unimportant city.

EUROPE DISCOVERS TIMBUKTU

People in Europe didn't know the truth about Timbuktu. They didn't know it had grown poor. They still thought it was a city of gold.

The Sahara (or "Great Desert" in Arabic) covers most parts of northern Africa from the Red Sea in the east to the Atlantic Ocean in the west. The area of the desert is about 3,500,000 square miles (9,000,000 square km).

DID YOU *Know?*

The Sahara is larger than the continent of Australia. It is almost as big as the United States. It measures more than 3.5 million square miles (9 million sq. km) in area. It covers most of northern Africa. The Sahara is one of the harshest regions on Earth. In daytime, temperatures can soar to 136°F (58°C). At night, temperatures can dip to 22°F (–6°C).

To prepare for his expedition to Timbuktu in 1827–1828, René Caillié (below) *spent eight months in Senegal in western Africa learning Arabic and the laws and customs of Islam.* Bottom: *A view of Timbuktu in 1879, fifty years after Caillié's visit*

European merchants wanted to get some of that gold for themselves. They wanted to trade with Timbuktu.

During the 1700s and early 1800s, European explorers tried to reach Timbuktu. But getting to Timbuktu from Europe was not easy. Explorers had to travel through the Sahara, the world's largest desert. And they had to do it twice—once when going to Timbuktu and again when returning home. Explorers often ran out of water in the desert. They also faced starvation, disease, and accidents. Hostile desert people sometimes attacked and killed unknown travelers. Many Europeans gave up before reaching Timbuktu.

The first European to make it to Timbuktu and back was René Caillié. In the 1820s, this French explorer traveled to western Africa. He disguised himself as a Muslim so as not to anger the local people.

When he reached Timbuktu, he was amazed at what he found. Rather than a city

of gold, Caillié found a poor and run-down town. "I had a totally different idea of the grandeur and wealth of Timbuctoo," he wrote. "The city presented, at first site, nothing but a mass of ill-looking houses, built of earth. Nothing was to be seen in all directions, but immense quicksands of yellowish white color . . . the most profound silence prevailed." People in Europe were disappointed to learn the truth about Timbuktu.

A MODERN WONDER

In modern times, Timbuktu is part of the Republic of Mali. Mali is one of the poorest countries in the world.

In Timbuktu the gold is all gone. Many of the city's thirty thousand people are poor. But Timbuktu still has three big mosques and a university. It has libraries full of valuable old manuscripts. Many talented writers, artists, and musicians make their home in Timbuktu. The city is also a UNESCO World Heritage Site. Although the gold is gone, visitors to the city can still see reminders of its past glory.

THE TIMBUKTU Manuscripts

Ancient Timbuktu was a center of Islamic learning. It had libraries full of manuscripts. The manuscripts were handwritten in Arabic, the language of Islamic scholars. In modern times, about seven hundred thousand ancient manuscripts still remain in Timbuktu. The manuscripts are kept in public and private libraries. They cover topics such as mathematics, chemistry, astronomy, medicine, history, and religion. Many of the manuscripts are in danger of being lost. Age has made their pages brittle. The paper crumbles when it's touched. Insects, moisture, and mold have also damaged the manuscripts. Officials in Timbuktu are collecting money to preserve the manuscripts and store them in better conditions.

Modern residents of Timbuktu walk past the Sankore Mosque.

CHOOSE AN EIGHTH WONDER

Now that you've read about the seven wonders of ancient Africa, do a little research to choose an eighth wonder. Or make a list with your friends and vote to see which wonder is the favorite.

To do your research, look at some of the websites and books listed in the Further Reading and Websites sections of this book. Look for places in Africa that
- *have a cool history*
- *were difficult to make at the time or required new technology*
- *were extra big or tall*
- *were hidden from view or unknown to foreigners for many centuries*

You might even try gathering photos and writing your own chapter on the eighth wonder!

TIMELINE

2 MILLION B.C.	The ancestors of modern humans live in Africa.
3000 B.C.	Ancient civilization begins in Africa when rulers start forming kingdoms.
2500s B.C.	The pharaoh Khafre reigns in Egypt. He builds the Great Sphinx.
2400s B.C.	The Nubians develop a kingdom along the Nile River south of Egypt.
1200s B.C.	Pharaoh Ramses II builds Abu Simbel in honor of himself and his wife.
1000 B.C.	The kingdom of Kush emerges in Nubia, south of Egypt.
A.D. 100	The kingdom of Aksum develops in northeastern Africa.
900	The Swahili coast becomes a major trading center.
1000	Southern Africans begin building the city of Mapungubwe.
1100s	The Shona people begin building Great Zimbabwe. A settlement begins at Timbuktu in Mali.
1235	A leader named Sundiata creates the kingdom of Mali.
1307	Mansa Musa becomes the ruler of Mali.
1497	The Portuguese explorer Vasco da Gama discovers thriving cities along the Swahili coast.
EARLY 1500s	Portuguese traders discover Great Zimbabwe.
	French scientists begin to excavate and study the Great Sphinx.
1813	Swiss explorer Johann Burckhardt finds Abu Simbel buried in the sand.
1816	Italian archaeologist Giovanni Battista Caviglia completes excavations of the Great Sphinx.
1817	Giovanni Battista Belzoni explores the Great Temple at Abu Simbel.
1828	French explorer René Caillié becomes the first European to reach Timbuktu and return to Europe.
1932	Archaeologists discover the ruins of Mapungubwe in southern Africa.
1960s	Work begins on the Aswan High Dam across the Nile River. Workers rescue Kushite artifacts from the floodwaters. They move Abu Simbel and other structures to higher ground.
2007	Ethiopia plans to set up a stela from ancient Aksum. The stela had been in Rome for seventy years.

GLOSSARY AND PRONUNCIATION GUIDE

Abu Simbel: ah-boo SIHM-bel

afterlife: life after death

Aksum: ahk-SOOM

archaeologists: scientists who study buildings, tools, and other remains of ancient cultures

artifacts: statues, tools, weapons, and other objects remaining from ancient cultures

desert: a region with little rainfall and sparse vegetation. Many deserts also have hot climates.

excavate: to dig up artifacts or structures that have been buried by dirt, rock, and sand

griot (GREE-oh): an African storyteller who memorizes and relates history as legends, poems, and songs

hieroglyphics: a system of picture writing from ancient Egypt

Islam: a major world religion, founded on the Arabian Peninsula (modern-day Saudi Arabia) in the A.D. 600s

Kush: kush

monolith: a monument or carving made from a single piece of stone

monument: a building, large statue, or other large structure

mortar: a building material placed between stones or bricks. When it hardens, mortar glues the blocks together tightly.

mosque: an Islamic house of worship

mummy: a dead body that has been preserved, either by natural processes or by human preservation techniques

pharaoh (FAYR-oh): a king of ancient Egypt

pyramid: a large, ancient structure with four triangular walls that meet at a point on top

ruins: the remains of a destroyed city or group of buildings

Sphinx: sfihnks

stelae (STEE-lee): tall, thin, four-sided monuments used in Aksum to mark the location of royal tombs

Swahili: swah-HEE-lee

Timbuktu: tihm-buhk-TOO

Zimbabwe: zihm-BAH-bway

SOURCE NOTES

11 Christopher Berg, "The Great Sphinx and the Glimmering Light of History," *Amazingart.com*, 2004, http://www.amazeingart.com/seven-wonders/sphinx.html (February 7, 2007).

13 Jimmy Dunn, "Tuthmosis VI of the 18th Dynasty," *Tour Egypt*, 2003, http://www.touregypt.net/featurestories/tuthmosis4.htm (January 26, 2007).

17 Ascending Passage, "The Rameses Temple at Abu Simbel," *AscendingPassage.com*, 2006, http://ascendingpassage.com/N-14-Abu-Simbel-Ramesses.htm (January 10, 2007).

18 BookRags, "Science and Its Times—on the Temples at Abu Simbel," *BooksRags*, 2006, http://www.bookrags.com/Abu_Simbel (January 13, 2007).

21 BookRags, "The Temples at Abu Simbel," *BookRags*, 2006, http://www.bookrags.com/research/the-temples-at-abu-simbel-scit-051/ (February 19, 2007).

21 Charles Leonard Irby and James Mangles, "Departure for Abou-Simbel," *Travellers in Egypt*, n.d., http://www.travellersinegypt.org/archives/2004/09/departure_for _abousimbel.html (February 18, 2007).

22 Percy Bysshe Shelley, "Ozymandias," *The Literature Network*, 2007, http://www.online-literature.com/shelley_percy/672/ (November 7, 2007).

22 *New York Times*, "First Egyptian Record of Snow Is Discovered: Word Found by Prof. Breasted in the Temple of Abu Simbel," October 18, 1906, A14.

28 Tormud Eide, Tomas Hägg, Richard Holton Pierce, and László Török, eds., *Fontes Historiae Nubiorum. Textual Sources for the History of the Middle Nile Region between the Eighth Century BC and the Sixth Century AD* (Bergen, NO: University of Bergen, 1994), 3:840–845.

31 Ibid., 1:326.

36 Paul Halsall, "The Periplus of the Erythraean Sea: Travel and Trade in the Indian Ocean by a Merchant of the First Century," *Ancient History Sourcebook*, October 2000, http://www.fordham.edu/halsall/ancient/periplus.html (October 19, 2007).

38 Stuart Munro-Hay, "The Royal Tombs of Aksum," *About.com: Archaeology*, 1991, http://archaeology.about.com/od/ironage/ig/The-Royal-Tombs-of-Aksum/Excavating-Axum .htm (November 12, 2007).

44 BBC, "The Story of Africa: The Swahili," *BBC World Service*, n.d., http://www.bbc .co.uk/worldservice/africa/features/storyofafrica/5chapter3.shtml (January 5, 2007).

45 Halsall.

45 Ibid.

46 ORIAS, "Monsoon Winds to the 'Land of Gold,'" *Office of Resources for International and Areas Studies*, August 2007, http://ias.berkeley.edu/orias/spice/textobjects/primary _sources.htm (February 19, 2007).

52 Richard Effland, Dave Turkon, and Alan Levine, "Slide Show," *Mesa Community College*, June 18, 2003, http://www.mc.maricopa.edu/~reffland/anthropology/anthro2003/legacy/africa/zimbabwe (January 22, 2007).

54 Roderick J. Mcintosh, "Riddle of Great Zimbabwe," *Archaeology*, July/August 1998, http://www.archaeology.org/9807/abstracts/africa.html (January 22, 2007).

63 Africa Travel Association, "Tombouctou, Mysterious City of Mali, West Africa," *Africa Travel Association*, 2006, http://www.africa-ata.org/tombouctou.htm (December 31, 2006).

63–64 Al-Bakri, "Kingdom of Ghana, Primary Source Documents," *Boston University, African Studies Center*, March 2005, http://www.bu.edu/africa/outreach/materials/handouts/k_o_ghana.html (February 10, 2007).

64 George Glazer Gallery, "The Catalan Atlas—19th c. Edition in 6 Maps," *George Glazer Gallery*, 2006, https://www.georgeglazer.com/maps/world/catalanenane.html (January 7, 2007).

68 René Caillié, *Travels through Central Africa to Timbuctoo*, vol. 2 (London: H. Colburn & R. Bentley, 1830), 49.

SELECTED BIBLIOGRAPHY

Bahn, Paul G., ed. *Cambridge Illustrated History: Archaeology*. Cambridge: Cambridge University Press, 1996.

Burton, Rosemary, and Richard Cavendish. *Wonders of the World: 100 Great Man-Made Treasures of Civilization*. New York: Metro Books, 2003.

Cantor, Norman F. *Antiquity: The Civilization of the Ancient World*. New York: HarperCollins, 2003.

De Villiers, Marq, and Sheila Hirtle. *Into Africa: A Journey through the Ancient Empires*. Toronto: Key Porter Books, 1997.

Hanbury-Tenison, Robin. *The Oxford Book of Exploration*. New York: Oxford University Press, 1993.

Hancock, Graham, and Santha Faiia. *Heaven's Mirror: Quest for the Lost Civilization*. New York: Crown Publishers, 1998.

Kryza, Frank T. *The Race for Timbuktu: In Search of Africa's City of Gold*. New York: HarperCollins, 2006.

Renfrew, Lord, and Paul G. Bahn, eds. *The Cambridge Illustrated History of Archaeology*. Cambridge: Cambridge University Press, 1999.

Scarre, Chris, ed. *The Seventy Wonders of the Ancient World: The Great Monuments and How They Were Built*. London: Thames and Hudson, 2000.

Stefoff, Rebecca. *Finding the Lost Cities*. New York: Oxford University Press, 1997.

Tyldesley, Joyce. *Egypt: How a Civilization Was Rediscovered*. Berkeley: University of California Press, 2005.

Waldman, Carl, and Alan Wexler. *Who Was Who in World Exploration*. New York: Facts on File, 1992.

Westwood, Jennifer. *Atlas of Mysterious Places*. London: Marshall Editions, 1987.

FURTHER READING AND WEBSITES

Books and Magazines

Brook, Larry. *Daily Life in Ancient and Modern Timbuktu*. Minneapolis: Lerner Publications Company, 1999. This book traces the history of the city known as the Pearl of Africa—from its origins to modern times.

Day, Nancy. *Your Travel Guide to Ancient Egypt*. Minneapolis: Twenty-First Century Books, 2001. This book takes readers on a tour of ancient Egypt. What did the ancient Egyptians wear? What did they eat? How did they travel? Readers will find out in this handy guide.

DiPiazza, Francesca. *Mali in Pictures*. Minneapolis: Twenty-First Century Books, 2007. From ancient times to the twenty-first century, Mali has a fascinating story. This book looks at the nation's history, culture, landscape, and economy.

——. *Zimbabwe in Pictures*. Minneapolis: Twenty-First Century Books, 2005. The author examines Zimbabwe from all angles—history, geography, society, economy, and culture. She explores the attractions of this ancient nation, including Great Zimbabwe.

Fontes, Ron, and Justine Fontes. *Sunjata: Warrior King of Mali*. Minneapolis: Graphic Universe, 2008. Sunjata (or Sundiata) was a powerful western African king. This graphic novel tells his story in words and pictures.

Giblin, James Cross. *Secrets of the Sphinx*. New York: Scholastic Press, 2004. The author examines the ins and outs of the Great Sphinx at Giza: When and how was it built? What can it tell us about ancient Egypt? What are scientists doing to protect this precious wonder? Gorgeous full-color illustrations add to the book's appeal.

McKissack, Patricia, and Frederick McKissack. *The Royal Kingdoms of Ghana, Mali and Songhay: Life in Medieval Africa*. New York: Henry Holt and Company, 1994. The McKissacks provide a comprehensive overview of the great kingdoms of Ghana, Mali, and Songhai. The book is a well-researched and user-friendly introduction to these kingdoms.

Sherrow, Victoria. *Ancient Africa: Archaeology Unlocks the Secrets of Africa's Past*. New York: National Geographic Children's Books, 2007. New technologies are helping archaeologists study the wonders of ancient Africa. This book from the National Geographic Society reveals the latest discoveries.

Sonneborn, Liz. *The Ancient Kushites*. New York: Franklin Watts, 2005. Ancient Kush was a magnificent empire in northern Africa, yet few people know of its splendors. In this book, Sonneborn sheds light on this little-known kingdom and its people.

Websites

Civilizations in Africa: Axum

http://www.wsu.edu:8080/~dee/CIVAFRCA/AXUM.HTM

This site teaches visitors about the wonders of ancient Aksum (also spelled Axum). You can scroll though the menu bar to learn about other African civilizations as well.

Geographica

http://www.geographia.com/

This website provides information about the nations of the world. Click on "Africa" to learn more about Mali, Zimbabwe, and other African nations.

Kids Zone: The Countries of Africa

http://www.afro.com/children/discover/discover.html

This site teaches students about the wonders of Africa. It includes myths, games, brainteasers, and an interactive map.

The Story of Africa

http://www.bbc.co.uk/worldservice/africa/features/storyofafrica/index.shtml

The British Broadcasting Corporation developed this site about the civilizations of Africa in earlier centuries.

vgsbooks.com

http://www.vgsbooks.com

Visit www.vgsbooks.com for links to all sorts of useful information about African countries, including geographical, historical, demographic, cultural, and economic websites. The vgsbooks.com site is also a great resource for late-breaking news and statistics about the nations of Africa.

Wonders of the African World

http://www.pbs.org/wonders/index.html

This site from the Public Broadcasting System introduces the history and cultures of ancient cities in Africa.

INDEX